The Sustainable Landscape

Recycling Materials
Water Conservation

Damon Lang
With Darlene Claire Preussner

Schiffer Publishing Ltd
4880 Lower Valley Road, Atglen, PA 19310

Other Schiffer Books By The Author:
New Ideas for Living Outdoors, 978-0-7643-3533-4, $24.99

Other Schiffer Books on Related Subjects:
International Award-Winning Pools, Spas & Water Environments, 978-0-7643-3480-1, $24.99
Hot Tubs & Spas: An Inspirational Design Guide, 0-7643-1841-1, $24.95

Library of Congress Control Number: 2010923337

Designed by John P. Cheek
Cover design by Bruce Waters

Type set in Trajan Pro/Zurich BT

ISBN: 978-0-7643-3452-8
Printed in China

Designs and installations by Damon Lang and Green Planet Landscaping. "A River Runs Through" pool by LGP.

Photography by Damon Lang, Louie Traub, Rosalyn Putnam, Gary McCreary, and Eryn Ence.

Staging by Darlene Claire Preussner, Gary McCreary, Rosalyn Putnam, and Jenny Stallings.

Project key and plant material pages by Edgar Herrera.

DEDICATION

To Lawrence and Jean Lang, my wonderful parents, for all your love and support.

To Mama Green, who passed before this book was printed. Her favorite part was the dedication, so this one's for you.

Schiffer Books are available at special discounts for bulk purchases for sales promotions or premiums. Special editions, including personalized covers, corporate imprints, and excerpts can be created in large quantities for special needs. For more information contact the publisher:

Published by Schiffer Publishing Ltd.
4880 Lower Valley Road
Atglen, PA 19310
Phone: (610) 593-1777; Fax: (610) 593-2002
E-mail: Info@schifferbooks.com

For the largest selection of fine reference books on this and related subjects, please visit our web site at **www.schifferbooks.com**
We are always looking for people to write books on new and related subjects. If you have an idea for a book please contact us at the above address.

This book may be purchased from the publisher.
Include $5.00 for shipping.
Please try your bookstore first.
You may write for a free catalog.

In Europe, Schiffer books are distributed by
Bushwood Books
6 Marksbury Ave.
Kew Gardens
Surrey TW9 4JF England
Phone: 44 (0) 20 8392 8585; Fax: 44 (0) 20 8392 9876
E-mail: info@bushwoodbooks.co.uk
Website: www.bushwoodbooks.co.uk

CONTENTS

Acknowledgments

First, I want to thank my parents for their patience, guidance, and support. I thank my brothers and sisters-in-law for sharing laughter and love. I thank Sophie and Scotty for bringing a smile to my face by having fun. I could not have a better family. I love you and thank you all.

To my clients for allowing my vision of their dreams to become reality and the GPL team for their hard work and dedication.

To Darlene for her hard work and determination to complete this book. I cannot thank you enough for your beautiful words. Linda, I want you to know you are an asset. I appreciate everything you have done.

I thank Gary, my best friend and confidant. I can never thank you enough for all you have done for me.

And to Roz, Louie, and Eryn for capturing the spirit and personality of the projects with beautiful images. I thank Roz and Tyler for friendship that could not have come at a better time. Roz, I enjoyed the time we all spent together and I'm really going to miss that.

—Damon Lang

INTRODUCTION

We have all heard the expression, "going green," and the words "recycled" and "sustainability" are now in common use. Will they be here today and gone tomorrow? Let's hope not.

Protecting the environment is a responsibility we all share. The projects presented in this book apply methods of water efficiency and incorporate the use of recycled materials.

In the Southwest, natural resources are scarce. The Colorado River system is facing the worst drought on record. As a result, governing agencies are enacting and enforcing watering restrictions and conservation measures. Resistance is waning and communities have learned to live in compliance.

Xeriscaping, a term commonly used to describe desert landscaping, is actually a water conservation method that can be applied to every garden style. Established by a Denver, Colorado, task force, Xeriscaping combines planning and design, soil improvement, appropriate plant selection, practical turf areas, efficient irrigation, use of mulches, and regular maintenance. The outcome is a beautiful landscape that consumes less water.

Equally important is the selection of materials that are non-toxic, recycled, and resource efficient. Durable products last longer and therefore need to be replaced less often. Concrete flooring is environmentally sensitive since it is not mined, cut down, kiln dried, or synthesized, and there is virtually no waste. Trex™ is a wood substitute made of reclaimed wood and plastic. It is sturdy, long-lasting, maintenance free, not to mention attractive and affordable. Synthetic turf is available for those who want the appearance of a lush green lawn. Manufacturers now offer products that look and feel natural in any region and come with a warranty of up to a decade.

Nature deserves our respect. Protecting the environment should be more than just a concept, but a way of life. To live in harmony with the planet, consider the words of an Iroquois tribal leader: "With every decision we make, we keep in mind the seventh generation to come. It is our job to see that the people coming ahead have a world no worse than ours and hopefully better. When we walk on Mother Earth we always plant our feet carefully because we know the faces of our future generations are looking up at us from beneath the ground. We never forget them." One can only hope.

NO PARKING FIRE LANE
ADT

Escape the Ordinary

Everyone needs a place to unwind, clear their mind, and cleanse their soul. A well-designed, private retreat incorporates details that reflect the owner's personality and style. Exhibiting playful sophistication and undeniable charm, this outdoor living space touches the kindred spirit in all of us.

Visible to guests entering the front door, the pool's stunning water feature is the centerpiece of the backyard. Flanked by columns of stacked stone crowned with blazing fire bowls, water sheers from the top of a tiled wall—appearing to pour directly onto the fire pit centered below.

At second glance the optical illusion is revealed. The flames are coming from a matching fire bowl atop a pedestal surrounded by a sunken bench. This entices the visitor to explore the exterior of the house to look for other hidden visual treasures.

You feel energized the instant you step into the backyard. Separate activity areas, connected by recurring patterns in the flooring material, are alive with eye-catching color combinations and whimsical personal touches.

A vibrant scarlet umbrella hovers over an 8", raised Trex deck resembling natural redwood flooring. Beautifully detailed with diamond shaped glass medallions and mosaic, glass tile, a spa awaits. Precariously perched, as if ready to dive in the warm water, is a handcrafted parrot ornament.

Journey to the other side of the property and you step up to a lively space for socializing, anchored by a unique concave fireplace. Shaped to match the multi-leveled patio it hosts, the feature is capped with a stone overmantle, shelf, and extended hearth. The stucco facade is painted in an unexpected palette of purple and green. Sitting on the raised, built in bench, the words "Dream", "Imagine", and "Believe" grab your attention.

As you survey the yard and absorb all the sights and sounds it offers, your heart becomes light, your mind free, your spirit unleashed, and your body relaxed. Closing your eyes, the desire for a private sanctuary expressive of your personality is overwhelming. That's when it hits you like a ton of bricks. All you have to do is dream, imagine, and believe.

Visible to guests entering the front door, a stunning water feature is the centerpiece of the yard.

Before images.

Glass tile mosaics and vibrant colors accent water, fire features, and the steps of the pool.

Tall bamboo branches in decorative pots add vertical dimension.

Bench seating surrounds a pedestal fire pit.

Fire pits are a great way to spark romance.

Recycled, tempered glass sparkles even when the fire pit is not ablaze.

Ornamental objects bring color and character to personalize the space.

The glass tile mantle shows off the homeowner's treasures.

Eye catching color combinations and decorative accents make this fireplace distinctive.

An elevated Trex deck patio hosts an ideal gathering spot to enjoy the fireplace.

The blaze within the fireplace casts a warm glow throughout the yard.

PROJECT KEY

1. TREX ™ DECK
2. 1"X1" RECYCLED GLASS TILE
3. LIGHT STREAMS ™ GLASS TILE
4. 3M™ QUARTZ PLASTER
5. RECYCLED GLASS CHIPS
6. STAINED FIREBRICK
7. FABRIQUE™ 1'X1' GRIS LINEN
8. LIME GREEN STUCCO FACE
9. FLAGSTONE CAP

Resting atop an 8", raised Trex deck, the enticing spa can be both invigorating and relaxing.

Beautiful glass tile mosaics accent the spa.

The slats of the Trex deck are in perfect alignment with the glass tile mosaic of the spa.

The symmetrical design creates an optical illusion for guests arriving at the front door.

Comfortable furniture invites guests to stay and enjoy the relaxing atmosphere.

Protected from the elements beneath the covered patio, guests can converse and take in the scenery.

Pouring from the top of a wall, bursting from a center bubbler, and cascading into the pool, the melodic sounds of water in motion mask unwanted noise and produce a calming effect.

Natural, stacked stone faces on the columns flanking the water feature.

The sights and sounds of the water feature can be appreciated while seated around the warming fire pit.

Bench seating below the water feature hosts an aquatic audience.

Underwater LED lighting allows nighttime viewing of the water feature.

Varying surface materials and intricate flooring patterns create interest.

Mondo grass planted in river rock creates an interesting pattern and divides various activity areas.

Hanging lanterns provide low-voltage illumination to pathways.

Recessed lighting assures safe steps out into the night.

Lighting can cast subtle shadows, highlight design features, and ensure enjoyment well after dark.

The setting sun creates myriad colors across the yard.

PROJECT KEY

1. 1/2″ RIVER ROCK
2. BRONZE LOUVER LIGHT
3. SAND FINISH CONCRETE STEPS
4. S/S UMBRELLA SLEEVE
5. RECYCLED GLASS
6. DECORATIVE PIECE
7. PAVESTONE™ PAVERS
8. PRO-FIT™ STONE
9. 6″X6″ PORCELAIN TILE
10. SHEER DESCENT
11. BUBBLER
12. BLACK COPPER METAL POT
13. LOW PROFILE FIRE WOK BOWL

PLANT MATERIALS

1. RADIATION LANTANA
2. FORTNIGHT LILY
3. TRUMPET VINE
4. BOUGAINVILLEA
5. BUTTERFLY BUSH
6. STATICE PLANT
7. DOUBLE KNOCKOUT® ROSE BUSH

Moody Blue

Cool shades of blue and the soothing sounds of water generate the ideal atmosphere for entertaining guests, socializing with friends, or escaping for a romantic interlude. Through subtle manipulation, the homeowners can alter the backyard's surroundings to satisfy their ever-changing moods.

Located just steps away from the indoor kitchen is the outdoor beverage center. An illuminated onyx bartop is a stylish way to accommodate guests. For the more adventurous, seating is available at the swim-up bar or the handsomely inlaid floating table. The sunken outdoor kitchen has all the amenities and allows for the preparation and service of poolside refreshments. Vibrant red umbrellas cast necessary shade and offer contrasting colors.

A variety of visual and auditory stimulation is achieved remotely with the touch of a button, whether it's the calming effect of a sheer rain descent, or the exhilaration of an erupting spa.

Tucked around the corner, waiting to be discovered, is a fire and water feature surrounded by sofa-style seating. Water spills over iridescent glass tile, highlighted by the flames flickering in a bowl floating on top.

Whether satisfying a mood, instilling an emotion, or setting a tone, the end result of this backyard design is a pleasurable one.

Shades of blue create the perfect mood for pleasure.

Before images.

River rock washed with subtle hues of blue separate the Trex stepping pads and travertine pavers.

Perfect around pools, travertine pavers absorb less heat.

Stone blue, sand finish concrete is a durable and attractive flooring choice.

Retaining walls of azure and aqua filled with native plant material mimic the earth and sky.

Bamboo reaches for the pool from a built-in planter.

A 24", raised bond beam is capped with sand finish concrete.

Another area for entertaining is inconspicuously tucked away on the side of the house.

Shaded by a scarlet umbrella, guests can soak in the crystal clear water of the spa.

Stainless steel scuppers spill cool water into the pool.

The spa sits perfectly symmetrical to the angular "V"-shaped scuppers.

A sheer descent rains down, creating yet another hue of blue.

Lay back on the floating bed and listen to the relaxing sound of water pouring from the scuppers.

Sofa-style seating accommodates the relaxing effect of the fire and water feature.

Appearing to float, a glass pan holds the fire element, anticipating darkness.

Water spills gently over the shimmering iridescent glass tile.

Bougainvilleas add vibrant splashes of color.

Glass tile mosaics are a decorative detail found throughout the yard.

A vibrant red umbrella shades the lounging area.

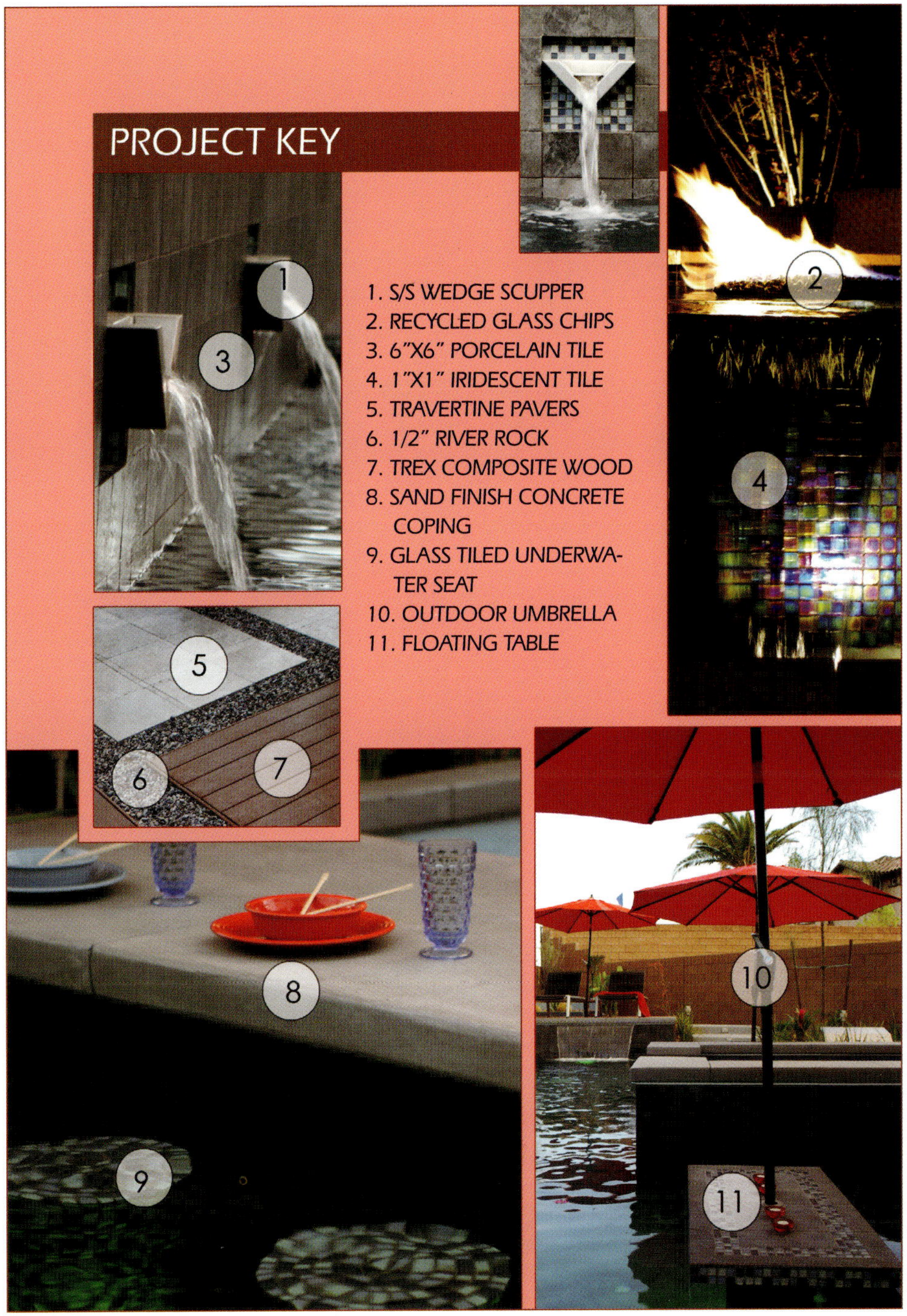

An elevated lounging area is perched above the outdoor kitchen and pool.

Steep steps reveal the depth of the kitchen.

Prepare meals poolside in the full kitchen.

Stainless steel appliances are durable and attractive.

An opening under the counter provides another storage option.

Above a storage niche in the sunken kitchen, a fresh herb garden awaits the chef.

The refreshment center is conveniently located near the indoor kitchen.

A cocktail pro cooler makes bartending a breeze.

A bar top of beautiful translucent onyx becomes more dynamic with LED lights mounted underneath.

The refreshment center is supported by a single leg.

Used mainly as flooring, Trex materials also make a lovely skirt.

Protected by a crimson umbrella, a floating table makes the perfect setting for an aquatic rendezvous for two.

Underwater seating is also available at the swim-up countertop.

Submersible fixtures focus attention on the prismatic glass tile.

LED lights glow under water.

Stainless steel lighting was chosen for its reflective quality.

Lights recessed into the steps allow for safe passage at night.

Colored lights create a mood that's anything but blue.

PROJECT KEY

1. ONYX COUNTERTOP
2. SAND FINISH CONCRETE COUNTER
3. TREX DECK SUPPORT
4. HERB PLANTER
5. 6" X 6" ASIAN BLACK TILE
6. SKY BLUE STUCCO FINISH
7. MOSAIC GLASS TILE 8. STORAGE NOOK
9. 4-BURNER TURBO™ GRILL W/PRO SEAR
10. OUTDOOR SINK
11. 2-DRAWER PAPER TOWEL
12. TRASH DRAWER
13. ACCESS DOOR
14. REFRIGERATOR

PLANT MATERIALS

1. LEMON TREE
2. VARIEGATED AGAVE
3. INDIAN FIG CACTUS
4. PINK CARPET ROSE
5. BOUGAINVILLEA VINE
6. ARTICHOKE AGAVE
7. RADIATION LANTANA
8. GREEN BAMBOO

Meditate & Rejuvenate

While some outdoor living spaces are utilized for entertaining and socializing, many homeowners seek a quiet retreat from everyday life. Simple and serene, this distinctive design incorporates separate elements to create an ideal refuge to relax, meditate, and rejuvenate.

The details in each element are duplicated throughout the space and are a unique way to infuse character, continuity, and clarity. A delicate balance of simplicity and dynamics, tranquility and stimulation, create an ideal personal escape to relax and recuperate.

Situated in one corner of the property for privacy, the glass tile spa beckons the weary to unwind in its warm circulating water. Pulsating jets massage soar muscles, relieve stress, and restore a sense of well-being.

Balancing the visual weight of the spascape is an elevated conversation and contemplation area, which is warmed by a fire pit. Located on the opposite side of the yard, vertical walls decorated with rich color, textured materials, and intricate patterns define the spatial dimensions, and make a statement all their own as a backdrop. Buddha sculptures elicit spirituality and encourage soul searching.

Enhancing the sights and sounds, centered in the landscape is the water feature. Pouring from spouts positioned at irregular levels, the melodic splashes of water to the basin below are amplified by the convex wall tiled with glass.

Contrasting colors evoke both calming and invigorating emotions.

Before images.

Varied plant material appeals to all five senses. *(Continued on following 2 pages)*

A shrine-like setting was erected for a Buddha statue.

Fire, one of natures most volatile elements, is honored next to the sacred statue.

Contrasting color backgrounds offset the opposing features.

Relax in the therapeutic churning water of the handsomely detailed spa.

The spa hosts the most relaxing views of the sunset.

Concrete creates smooth safe steps to the spa.

The concrete was acid stained in complimentary colors.

The Zen-like space is serene, orderly, and dedicated to meditation.

The red-hot, glass tile wall stands as a backdrop for the triple cannon scuppers.

Water benefits the area by eliminating distractions, promoting relaxation for the mind and body.

The curved inferno wall amplifies the sound of water and masks unwanted noise.

The water feature completes the circular theme.

Subtle lighting creates a calm environment for evening contemplation.

Trees are awash with flood lights.

Items of special significance are highlighted.

Properly installed, low-voltage lighting keeps the spa in seclusion.

Complimentary accents balance the contrasting features.

A recessed light in the floor illuminates the green panel wall.

Recycled glass chips reflect the radiance of the flames.

PROJECT KEY

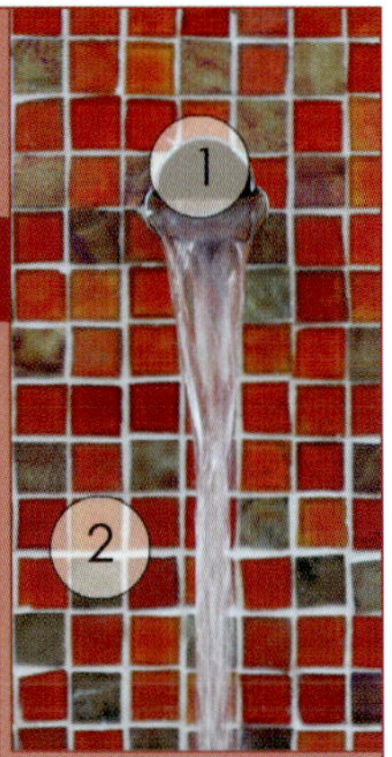

1. BRASS CANNON SCUPPER SPOUT
2. DISCO INFERNO GLASS TILE
3. COLOR COMBINATION RECYCLED GLASS CHIPS
4. OCEANSIDE™ GLASS TILE
5. FLAGSTONE CAP
6. OUTDOOR RECESSED LIGHT
7. CULTURED STONE™ VENEER
8. ACID STAINED CONCRETE

PLANT MATERIALS

1. LIME TREE
2. MEXICAN AGAVE
3. RED CARPET ROSE
4. FIG TREE
5. BRONZE FLAX
6. CAPE PLUMBAGO

Vacation Destination

Photography by Louie Traub

There is no denying that Southwestern summers are hot and dry. Temperatures reach triple digits for weeks on end with no relief in sight. That is, unless, you transform your backyard into a vacation getaway.

A sunken outdoor kitchen, fireplace, separate covered dining areas, and elevated spa make this the perfect place to stay and play.

It's easy to imagine you are on holiday in Florida when you enter this luxurious outdoor retreat. Dominated by white and shades ranging from cobalt to powder blue, the color palette is reminiscent of a seaside resort. A misting system overhead and hidden within the plant material provides the moisture necessary to recreate ocean breezes and lush landscaping.

The ultimate escape from the desert heat is to take a plunge in the cool, clear water of the pool. Surrounded by features that arch, bubble, pour, and rain down, the relaxing sounds and captivating sights of the animated water complete the tropical atmosphere. Enjoy the pleasures of eating, drinking, and viewing without leaving the water at the swim-up bar—seating is available just below the surface.

Transforming this backyard into the ultimate resort-style destination required a unique perspective.

Before images.

A lattice patio cover made of lightweight yet durable Alumawood™ offers relief from the sun.

The expansive patio cover traps the heat when it's cold and is wrapped with a mist system for the summer.

A mist system is also hidden in the vegetation, producing lush landscaping.

A sheer curtain of water drops to the turquoise pool below.

A mosaic glass tile wall amplifies the triple effect of falling water.

Arching fiber optic laminars produce dynamic aquatics.

Centered between dual fire bowls, the spa kindles romance.

Flames can intensify the mood.

The sizzling fire feature is mirrored in the aquamarine pool.

Caribbean-blue furniture comforts those viewing the fire and water display.

Resting on the cool green grass, a hammock is perfect for a long afternoon nap.

PROJECT KEY

1. ALUMAWOOD™ PATIO COVER
2. BUBBLERS-LED
3. S/S CURVED SCUPPERS
4. RECYCLED GLASS TILE
5. OBLIQUE SERIES™ LOW PROFILE FIRE BOWL
6. COLORED CONCRETE COPING
7. LED DECK LAMINAR
8. 3" X 3" PORCELAIN TILE
9. UNDERWATER SEATS

An elevated lounge area provides a relaxing vantage point.

Deluxe accommodations shelter the sunken open-air kitchen.

Accessories are stored within easy reach.

The sunken kitchen caters to guests at the swim-up bar.

Steps descend to the preparation area, below water level.

Intimate furnishings allow the cook to immediately relish the fruits of his labor.

Viewing and listening pleasures are satisfied by a state of the art surround sound system and LED flat panel televisions.

A separate dining area with a second flat panel television entertains large parties.

Centered between the kitchen and dining area, a fireplace permeates a warm glowing atmosphere.

Manufactured logs generate an authentic blaze within the fireplace.

PROJECT KEY

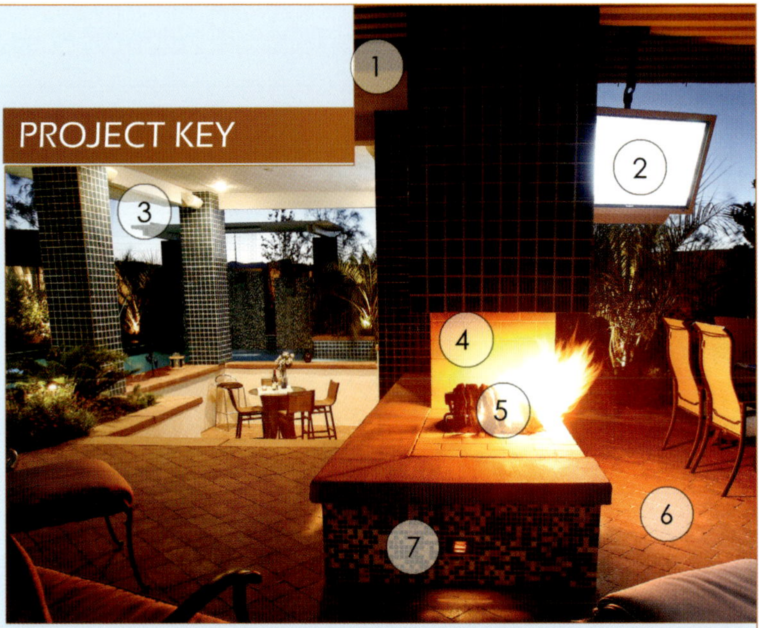

1. MIST SYSTEM
2. OUTDOOR FLAT SCREEN TV
3. RAIN DESCENT
4. FIRE BRICK
5. ARTIFICIAL FIRE LOGS
6. PAVESTONE TUMBLED PAVERS
7. RECYCLED GLASS TILE
8. KEGERATOR
9. REFRIGERATOR
10. 4-BURNER TURBO GRILL
11. WOOFER SPEAKER
12. S/S BBQ LIGHT
13. 2-DRAWER STORAGE
14. STUCCO FINISH
15. ELECTRIC PLUG
16. COCKTAIL PRO BAR

PLANT MATERIALS

1. PURPLE LEAF PLUM
2. RED YUCCA
3. PURPLE DAISY
4. HONEY SUCKLE
5. SAGO PALM
6. DWARF BOTTLEBRUSH

Seamless Transition

Today's outdoor living spaces have become an extension of the home, personalized with the style, taste, and character of its inhabitants. These homeowners gave the same attention to detail outside as they did to the interior design, and created an almost seamless transition from indoors to out.

Elegant travertine floors span the expansive covered dining area, first encountered when exiting the rear of the house. Stylish, comfortable furniture sets a relaxed atmosphere for socializing and entertaining. The kitchen is nestled between the support columns of the open-air room, fully equipped with a grill, refrigerator, storage, and towel drawers. There is also a natural limestone eating countertop to accommodate large dinner parties. Umbrella sleeves installed into the counter provide portable shelter from the elements and additional privacy from neighbors.

Anchoring the outdoor living room is a strong, cultured stone fireplace shouldered with broad mantles. Blazing logs in the wide firebox of this magnificent focal feature cast a warm glow and create a pleasant ambiance throughout the yard. Low, cushioned seating near the hearth creates a relaxed atmosphere for the intimate conversation area.

The flames from the fireplace are reflected on the still surface of the pristine pool, multiplying the dramatic effect of the contrasting elements. Surrounded by smooth travertine, the calm water provides added dimension to the open space, glimmering in the light, reflecting the sky above, and changing colors as day gives way to night. An elevated patio, tucked quietly at the distant end of the pool, makes the perfect destination for romantic stargazing.

Gathering in front of the fireplace is a tradition no longer limited to indoors.

Before images.

The wide variety of plant material appeals to all five senses. *(Continued on following page)*

A decorative urn of trailing plants softens the built-in storage nook.

Plant material can soften an area dominated by hardscape.

Plant material softens an exterior wall.

Synthetic turf serves as a natural cushion protecting the children's play area.

Adorned with mementos and handsomely detailed, it's easy to imagine this fireplace in any family room. The wide firebox allows more heat to escape.

Inlaid iridescent glass tile accents the stone fireplace.

The brilliant flames are reflected in the pool.

Travertine pavers make an elegant flooring transition from inside the home.

Raised ever so slightly, the therapeutic water of the spa awaits.

At the other end of the pool, the lounging area matches the elevation of the spa.

The glass tile accents on the spa step riser, between the travertine floor and matching bullnose coping, are repeated in the kitchen.

Viewed from the raised patio, the daytime sky bows to the moon and stars.

A secluded setting makes for romantic stargazing.

An expansive dining area is framed by the patio support columns, blanketed by soft warm light.

Faced with stone, the columns appear weighted.

An elegant wrought iron lamp creates the perfect ambiance.

An umbrella provides instant shade for the preparation area.

Low-voltage path and louver lights are an attractive source of safety and security.

Directional light adds a dramatic effect.

PROJECT KEY

1. CULTURED STONE VENEER
2. 2-DRAWER PAPER TOWEL
3. 4-BURNER GRILL
4. REFRIGERATOR
5. S/S LOUVER LIGHT
6. GLASS TILE
7. 2'X2' TRAVERTINE PAVERS
8. IRIDESCENT MOSAIC GLASS TILE
9. DECORATIVE URN
10. STORAGE BOX
11. CONCRETE MANTLE
12. LIMESTONE COUNTER-TOP W/CHISELED EDGE

PLANT MATERIALS

1. CAPE PLUMBAGO
2. PINEAPPLE SAGE
3. MEXICAN BIRD OF PARADISE
4. BUTTERFLY BUSH
5. BASIL
6. DWARF LIME TREE

Open-air Art Gallery

With modern outdoor living spaces, less is definitely more. The desire to eliminate excessive clutter and confusion translates into a simpler, cleaner, yet highly expressive landscape design. The homeowners are collectors and enthusiasts of unique handcrafted art and wanted their interests and individuality showcased in an open-air gallery used for entertaining, socializing, and relaxing.

The acid stained concrete flooring serves as the space's structural and aesthetic anchor, setting the tone with its rich, bold color. The comfortable, stately furniture is offset by the sleek surface and form, pattern, and texture emerge. The strong lines and geometric shapes are repeated throughout the area, creating an environmental work of art with imaginative displays of plant material in abstract concrete containers of contrasting colors.

Integrated into the rust-hued flooring, flagstone was used to draw visual attention to the iridescent glass tile fire table, mirroring the crescent-shaped planter it intersects. Colored to compliment the acid stain, the fire bowl atop the decorative feature makes a more dynamic statement of style at night as flames dance against the darkness. Dramatic low-voltage lighting casts intriguing profiles and mysterious shadows throughout the area.

The use of fewer materials and distinctive elements in the contemporary design result in an environmentally responsible, easily maintained work of living art.

A crescent moon hangs around the fire feature.

Before images.

Contrasting bluestone and cultured stone creates surface texture and appeal.

Matching stone veneer surfaces the built-in planters.

Abstract concrete containers hold fragrant displays, creating contemporary living art.

A solitary rocking chair makes a functional, artistic statement.

Sprinkles of color are repeated throughout the yard.

A tabletop fire bowl mimics the dining area beyond.

The fire table intersects a half-circle planter.

Fire safely erupts from the bowl, flames dancing against the darkening sky.

Vibrant, iridescent glass tiles reflect myriad colors.

The fire feature is a focal point, even from inside the home.

Savor a bottle of wine as the sun sets behind the distant mountain range.

A compact cooking center serves the dining area a few steps away.

Diners are treated to vast mountain views, one advantage of dining al fresco.

Clean lines and repeated patterns unify separate living spaces.

Acid-stained concrete makes a sleek—not slippery—stylish floor.

Inlaid flagstone embraces the central gathering spot.

Floating pads of concrete rest on synthetic turf.

Synthetic turf provides a water-wise carpet of green.

The overall appearance is clean and contemporary.

The abstract planters are given prominent lighting.

Outdoor lighting extends the hours of enjoyment well into the night.

PROJECT KEY

1. BLUESTONE INLAY
2. DECORATIVE POT
3. BLUESTONE CAP
4. BRONZE LOUVER LIGHT
5. CULTURED STONE VENEER
6. 1/2" RIVER ROCK
7. BBQ LIGHT
8. LYNX™ 3-BURNER GRILL
9. IRIDESCENT BASKET WEAVE GLASS TILE
10. RED 30" FIRE BOWL
11. ACID STAINED CONCRETE

PLANT MATERIALS

1. TRUMPET VINE
2. LEMON, LIVE, & CUMQUAT TREES
3. DWARF MYRTLE
4. FORTNIGHT LILY
5. ABELIA
6. YELLOW LANTANA

A River Runs Through

Photography by Louie Traub

Inspiration comes from a variety of sources. Developing the idea for the design of this project can be attributed, at least in part, to world renown architect Frank Lloyd Wright. A small-scale version of the master's work, Waterfall, the project unifies separate living spaces in a luxurious three-story home.

Guests to the magnificent home are captivated by the massive, imported palm trees planted in the front yard to balance the substantial size of the structure. Vegetation lines a staggered walkway leading to the courtyard. Gently cascading down a series of waterfalls, a babbling brook runs beside the house, beneath your feet, and under a walking bridge, which guides visitors to the front entrance.

Interior and exterior spaces are blended throughout the property. A grand family room, enclosed by three walls of glass, opens up to an elegant travertine tiled outdoor area with sweeping views of the mountains and the Las Vegas Strip.

The source of the stream that traverses through the house is visible as you encounter the fresh outdoor air. Stamped concrete that resembles wood bridges connect the various activity areas, including the pool, spa, outdoor kitchen, and fire pit. Strategically positioned for privacy, an outdoor bed offers romantic accommodations for sunbathing or stargazing.

A winding staircase descends to a tranquil Zen garden accessible from the lowest level of the home. Floating pads infused with river rock play host to an immense Buddha fountain. The trickling water adds an air of serenity. Tall bamboo shoots in textured pots, yew pines, and ornamental grasses add the perfect Asian touch.

Inspired by a master, it was the imaginative use of design elements that completed the unique style of a majestic home where a river runs through.

A Buddha fountain exudes a spiritual calm for peaceful meditation.

Before images.

Bamboo, Japanese black pine, and mondo grass nurture the Asian influence. *(Continued on following page)*

Dry bamboo shoots add vertical dimension.

Varied plant materials also add color and texture.

The symbolic fountain elevates the spirit and eases the mind.

Water flows between the floating pads around the solemn statue.

A private inner sanctum opens up to the sacred space.

From the top of a spiral staircase, the Zen area appears tranquil.

The fire pit is located close to the outdoor bed for romantic evenings.

The circular fire pit is capped with natural flagstone.

The pool looks as heavenly as the sky above.

The gentle, rounded slopes of the nearby mountains also influenced the shape of design elements.

The curves of the house are mirrored in the pool's surface and shape.

The sights and sounds of cascading water soothes the soul.

The rolling greens of a pristine golf course are just beyond the property.

The outdoor living area takes full advantage of the spectacular view.

The vista is framed by stone columns.

Massive imported palms balance the strong architecture.

The staggered walkway imitates the meandering stream, which is visible from the top step.

A river runs through separate living spaces in the home.

Natural boulders blend with man-made elements.

Nighttime lighting makes a grand statement.

PROJECT KEY

1. OUTDOOR BED
2. FLAGSTONE CAP
3. FIRE PIT W/ RECYCLED GLASS
4. IRIDESCENT TILE
5. DRY BAMBOO
6. SAND FINISH CONCRETE FLOATING PADS
7. 1/2" RIVER ROCK
8. JAPANESE LANTERN W/LED LIGHT
9. BEST QUALITY™ PATH LIGHT
10. BUDDHA FOUNTAIN

PLANT MATERIALS

1. MONDO GRASS
2. CANARY ISLAND DATE PALM
3. OCTOPUS AGAVE
4. PIGMY PALM
5. JAPANESE BLACK PINE
6. FOXTAIL FERN
7. SAGO PALM

Outdoor Room With A View

Photography by Louie Traub

Dividing their time between multiple residential properties, the homeowners mandated a low maintenance environment to make the most of the limited leisure area available. The design exceeds the demands—the result is the ultimate outdoor room with a view.

Situated high on a hilltop, the property offered spectacular views of the Las Vegas Strip in the distance and the pristine rolling greens of a golf course directly below. Planned open areas embraced the borrowed scenery, creating a sense of infinite space.

A lattice patio cover attached to the back of the house provides relief from the relentless desert sun while allowing much needed air circulation, which is generated by winds passing from the upper mountain to the lower basin.

Attractive, durable, environmentally sensitive, and easily maintained concrete was utilized to construct a multi-level, extended patio area for greater seating and viewing options.

Playing center stage to the outdoor room is a magnificent fire and water feature. Gently cascading down a half-circle, tiled wall, water accumulates in an illuminated trough. A fire bowl appears to magically float on top as the warmth of the flames are captured in the enclosure. The contrasting elements create a harmonious balance of light and sound.

Completing the virtually self-sustaining and ecologically responsible exterior living space was the installation of native plant material, synthetic turf, and low-voltage lighting.

The design incorporates qualities that require the minimum amount of care for the maximum amount of enjoyment in an outdoor room with a view.

An intense fire blazes against the night sky.

Before images.

Native plant material blends into the surrounding landscape.

Tall palm trees add vertical dimension and texture.

The undulating curves of the synthetic turf match those of the manicured greens on the golf course below.

The space extends the residents' lifestyle into the open-air.

Masked by vegetation, the outdoor room with a view is concealed from the front of the home.

The dual element feature is a focal point for the center of the space.

Appearing to float on top of the water, the fire bowl is mesmerizing.

On cool desert evenings, a toasty fire pit is the answer.

Seating is positioned to take full advantage of the dynamic fire and water feature and the vast view of the valley.

Separate seating areas are perched along the edge of the property.

Unobstructed views are guaranteed while dining at the lowest level of the outdoor room.

The mood and the table are set for dining al fresco.

Directional light profiles the tree against the night sky.

A soft and subtle tone is generated by low-voltage lighting.

Recessed louver lights allow for a safe descent to the lower patio area.

The setting sun washes hues of gold and orange over the landscape and mountains nearby.

The neon of the Las Vegas Strip illuminates the sky as the sun disappears.

PROJECT KEY

1. ALUMAWOOD PATIO COVER
2. PRE-CAST COLUMN
3. SAND FINISH CONCRETE
4. IRIDESCENT BASKET WEAVE RECYCLED GLASS TILE
5. LED AQUATIC LIGHTS
6. LARGE DECORATIVE RIVER ROCK
7. WIDE BOWL FIRE RING W/GLASS CHIPS
8. PRE-CAST CONCRETE FIRE BOWL

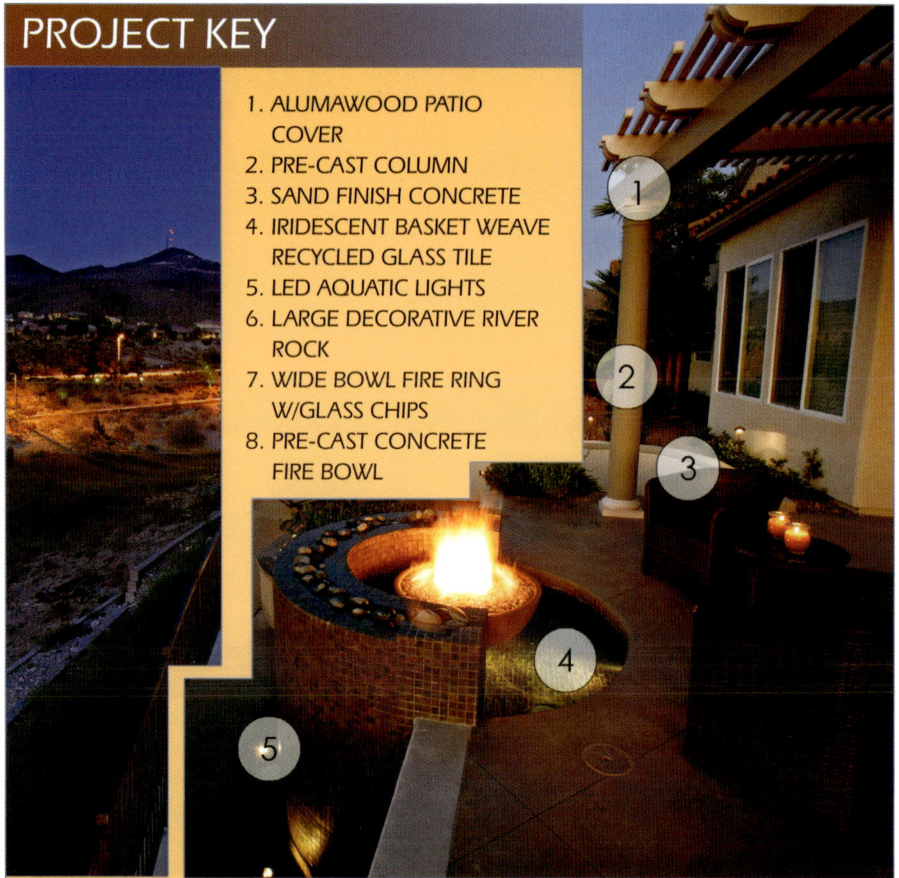

PLANT MATERIALS

1. CINNAMON BUNNY EAR CACTI
2. GOPHER PLANT
3. VARIEGATED AGAVE
4. PINK GROUND COVER ROSE
5. SOCIETY GARLIC
6. TEXAS RANGER
7. ARTICHOKE AGAVE

Modern Classic

Complementing the classic, timeless architecture of the home, the landscape design combines Old World charm with modern elements to create a reserved and relaxing outdoor environment.

Clipped hedges border a symmetrical paver stone walkway past a tiered formal fountain to the immense, arched front doorway. Stacked stone adorns the surfaces of columns at the entrance and rear of the house to match the home's facade, adding an air of antiquity. A detailed wall fountain graciously welcomes visitors taking the side path straight to the backyard.

The crisp, geometric shapes of the fire pit, spa, and swimming pool contribute to the formal style of the property. A lion's head scupper and age-old stone facing on the spa add timeless design elements in keeping with the classic architecture.

Modern features and details blend naturally with the traditional, increasing the visual interest and functionality overall. An ever-changing color wheel and fiber optic bubblers animate the infinity edge pool. Spilling over iridescent glass tile from the spa, a sheer water feature soothes with sound and motion.

Elegant furniture situated comfortably beneath a covered patio guarantees the homeowners can enjoy open-air dining after preparing a meal in the complete outdoor kitchen. Matching iridescent glass tile adorns the backsplash of the eating countertop, creating a sense of balance and unity.

Traditional and formal decorative accents and a disciplined use of modern elements and design details combine to make an unforgettably grand statement of style.

Water pouring from the lion's head scuppers to the pool bring gentle, splashing sounds to the yard.

Before images.

The mountain struggles to compete with the grand style of the home.

Low, clipped hedges and symmetrically patterned walkways infuse a classic style.

Carved grapes adorn a formal fountain in the courtyard.

The sights and sounds of water trickling from an ornate wall fountain can be enjoyed from the interior dining room.

Mouth agape, the lion's head scupper pours water.

The flames radiate warmth and light to the covered living space.

The dazzling flames are reflected in the sparkling water.

Classic architecture sets the formal style of the property.

Geometric planters crown the columns rising from the infinity edge.

Splashes of color make the area come to life.

Recessed louver lights allow safe passage from inside to out.

The kitchen area and the sheer descent of the water feature are detailed with glass tile mosaics.

The eating countertop also serves as an extended preparation surface.

PROJECT KEY

1. OBLIQUE SERIES™ PLANTER BOWL
2. PRE-FAB FOUNTAIN
3. LION HEAD SCUPPER
4. 6"X6" PORCELAIN TILE
5. OUTDOOR FIRE-PIT
6. PAVESTONE BRICK PAVERS
7. BBQ GRILL
8. REFRIGERATOR
9. STORAGE DRAWER
10. RECYCLED GLASS TILE
11. TRASH DRAWER
12. CULTURED STONE™ VENEER

PLANT MATERIALS

1. RADIATION LANTANA
2. VINCA
3. FRUITLESS OLIVE TREE SWAN HILL
4. MEDITERRANEAN FAN PALM
5. PURPLE VERBENA
6. DWARF BOTTLEBRUSH

All The Right Angles

The contemporary landscape design of this home is in stark contrast to the jagged outcropping of the Red Rock Canyon and the gentle sloping hills of the golf course, which serves as its backdrop. right angles found in every corner of the yard. The modern design of the backyard sets the landscape apart from the rustic natural beauty of the surrounding terrain.

A variety of materials are used to achieve straight, clean, and perpendicular lines intersecting at right angles throughout the property. Square and rectangular concrete pavers initiate a pattern, which can be found in the pool's mosaic, porcelain tile and in the cultured stone wall beyond.

Travertine tile on the columns add clean crisp lines for the "V"-shaped scuppers, which mirror the

A variety of materials intersect at right angles throughout the property.

Before images.

Water spills from "V"-shaped scuppers, perpendicular to the travertine tiled columns.

The right angles of the hardscape are continued into the yard.

Sealed flagstone was used for the countertop in the outdoor kitchen.

The outdoor kitchen and dining area are treated to the fire and water feature. *(Continued on following page)*

Clean, crisp lines are in sharp contrast to the rugged mountain range in the distance.

The searing red flame and cool blue water are a striking contrast.

Repeating form and color invoke a sense of balance.

Twilight is reflected in the water and flames.

PROJECT KEY

1. REVERSE INFINITY EDGE
2. "V"-SHAPED SCUPPER
3. 1'X1' TRAVERTINE TILE
4. COLORED CONCRETE
5. 4-BURNER BBQ GRILL
6. 2-DRAWER/PAPER TOWEL
7. REFRIGERATOR
8. COUNTER MOUNTED GRILL LIGHT
9. TRASH DRAWER
10. STAINLESS STEEL LOUVER LIGHT
11. PAVESTONE BRICK PAVERS
12. COLORED CONCRETE COPING
13. GLASS CHIPS/FIRE PIT
14. 1"X1" PORCELAIN TILE

PLANT MATERIALS

1. JAPANESE BLUEBERRY
2. DWARF MYRTLE
3. MEXICAN FAN PALM
4. SAGO PALM
5. GOLDEN EUONYMUS